THE GOSPEL ACCORDING TO WILD INDIGO

Crab Orchard Series in Poetry
Editor's Selection

T0164597

THE GOSPEL ACCORDING TO WILD INDIGO

POEMS BY
CYRUS CASSELLS

Crab Orchard Review &
Southern Illinois University Press
Carbondale

Southern Illinois University Press
www.siupress.com

21 20 19 18   4 3 2 1

The Crab Orchard Series in Poetry is a joint publishing venture
of Southern Illinois University Press and *Crab Orchard Review*.
This series has been made possible by the generous support of
the Office of the President of Southern Illinois University and
the Office of the Vice Chancellor for Academic Affairs and
Provost at Southern Illinois University Carbondale.

Editor of the Crab Orchard Series in Poetry: Jon Tribble

Cover illustration: *Silhouette against the Blue* (cropped),
watercolor painting, by John L. Mendoza, 2010

Library of Congress Cataloging-in-Publication Data
Names: Cassells, Cyrus, author.
Title: The gospel according to wild indigo / poems by Cyrus
Cassells.
Description: Carbondale : Crab Orchard Review & Southern
Illinois University Press, 2018. | Series: Crab Orchard Series
in Poetry
Identifiers: LCCN 2017035952 | ISBN 9780809336609
(paperback) | ISBN 9780809336616 (e-book)
Subjects: | BISAC: POETRY / American / General.
Classification: LCC PS3553.A7955 A6 2018 | DDC 811/.54—dc23
LC record available at https://lccn.loc.gov/2017035952

Printed on recycled paper. ♻

This paper meets the requirements of ANSI/NISO Z39.48-1992
(Permanence of Paper) ∞

CONTENTS

I.
THE GOSPEL
ACCORDING TO
WILD INDIGO

The pine-tree sweetens my body.
The white iris beautifies me.

—Wallace Stevens,
"In the Carolinas"

THE GOSPEL ACCORDING TO WILD INDIGO

I. Dayclean

Dayclean's the Gullah word
for the gala sun, the looked-for

melon, meticulous,
up-and-coming,

impossibly hale,
ecstatically gilding

the Canaan of marshlands,
Low Country cosmos of scurrying

punchclock crabs,
dauntless kingfishers, frolicking

estuary herons—
Dayclean caresses

the praise houses—
eoho, eoho—

A.'s boy-time tree house
nestled in a Galahad

ancient oak.
Gold takes the street musician's

dented coronet—
Why's he still up?

Why's he still playing?—
burnishes the early-bird fingers

on a Mount Pleasant porch,
tea-brown Merlin fingers

fashioning palmetto roses,
palmetto crosses—

Crab castle, Jew's harp,
foxglove, sea junk,

marsh bridge, stilt house,
the white of hominy

and fine-sifted flour;
Lady's Island, Cat Island,

Daufuskie, St. Helena . . .
Rummaging gold matter-of-factly

gleans them all—
shell colors and dories,

rugged shrimp-sellers
and wind-blessed reeds—

rapacious gold.
Dayclean, dayclean:

sun like a schoolgirl
eager for show-and-tell.

II. A Is for Augustus

On a glove-yellow morning
of gleaming oyster shells,

crow-carried mussels,
placid seagulls perched

in priest-gentle pines
like festive Christmas ornaments,

beside an alluring Sea Island beach,
I first met up-front A.—

Bring your high yellow self
over here!

The name's Augustus
but folks call me A.—

Like vying truants with never-fail
cat's-eye marbles,

in no time flat, we traded
lived-to-tell tales

of our rambunctious
"North Cackalacky" childhoods—

an invigorating banter laced
with a tattoo of lapping water.

Later, when brash Mr. A. bent,
in a lazybones glory,

to brush my lips for the first time,
a snatch-gossip gust

hurled his cracked-brimmed hat
into a busybody

chorus of reeds, an eager-to-hear
amen corner,

and he darted, almost doe-quick,
to retrieve

the rash, wayward owl
of his windblown hat:

in-a-rush Augustus of the cattails,
the Indian summer estuary.

III. A.'s Childhood

Dayclean:
the mornings were moss-laden

and muleheaded—
kingdom of consoling porch swings

and steeping sun tea,
kingdom of throat-slick okra—

the mornings were mudplay
and faux-cannonfire and a makeshift

fortress of spartina;
a Gullah flourish

of gathered starfish in an heirloom
sweetgrass basket—

If you weren't hawkeyed,
the tantalizing but turncoat sea

could pick your pockets,
the gypsy-fingered sea

(filched forever,
the ward-away-trouble cat bone,

beachfront boy, the careworn
buffalo nickel)—

Summoned in the first gold hours,
A.'s usually rakehell hands

alongside his robust grandmother's
were lima-shelling hands,

and the music,
the music of "how do" and "I recollect."

IV. The Pine-Tree Sweetens My Body

As pine needles coalesce
with bulrush and sweetgrass, Augustus,

to shore a cherished
Sea Island basket,

so it seems, the fortifying,
peace-granting pines

have been nonchalantly
woven into my days.

Out of childhood and enmeshing memory,
they appear:

co-dreamers,
immobile shepherds, surely.

From a precocious, roving boy's
avid-to-learn vantage,

not as supreme as a giraffe—oh no,
but just as heaven-reaching—

For the inveterate pines, perhaps,
the crab-ruled Low Country

marshes have always been
arresting theatres:

whatever was shouted or gasped
at jubilee, at the silverpoint

of the bridegroom's climax
or the baby's crowning,

they ably cached
in their commanding branches,

so that if I lay my Hardy Boy ear
to the telltale bark

(as I did the tobacco-scented
summer I was nine),

some long-dead singing
from vanished dooryards,

from cabins and heart-stopping fields
(supper-getting-ready songs

hummed in pie-cooking heat)
is still ensconced in the pine.

V. A Gullah Valentine (Nearabout Spring)

Augustus, what I'm gung-ho to praise:
Mount Pleasant aunties who quell

ghosts of *feet-don't-fail-me-now*,
ghosts of *if-you're-black-stay-back*,

specters of inglorious slaving ships
and wolf-tough phantoms,

savvy, okra-cooking grannies,
who daily keep the flame

for the always-present-tense glory
of living Gullah—

What I love: the loop the loop
of our intoxicating days;

shredded barbecue
in a Winn-Dixie plastic bucket

and your younger sister Marquetta's
buttered and peppered stone-ground grits;

the bull's-eye of the beguiling
compound words of Gullah:

dayclean for the brisk, new,
indomitable day;

daylean for the dash-away
light on Kiawah or Edisto;

bukruhbittle for a lording
white man's "superior" food;

the timeworn brick leviathan
of fabled Catfish Row,

and the long-dreaming,
Apollo-lofty

Angel Oak on John's Island—
Lord, we were spat on;

we were whipped
in a Sea Island school,

the soul-struck, still-scrappy locals
sing out, *but now us speak*

our Gullah proudly—
A true Gullah valentine

would surely have to feature
Low Country branches graced

with green and lion-colored glass,
sun-washed empties

(Dr. Pepper, Mountain Dew,
Chardonnay, Manischewitz . . .),

chockablock shrimp shacks,
lush, leafy chinquapins,

and "sugar, sugar,
how'd you get so fly!"—

A., I know you had the gumption
or nervy bravery to share

news of our pistol-hot love
with your pew-strict,

disowning father (a catastrophe!),
and boy, it hurts,

but even so, let's hail
our hard-to-hold-still,

nearabout-spring moments,
the way the magnanimous

Low Country moon rises
past our gunwale

and fashions an unfolding,
March-into-April fan

in the big, rippling night mirror
of the marina.

VI. *The Low Country Magazine*

It's a rousing dream that mirrors
the schoolhouse beauty of these days

alongside you in the Low Country:
The sweep of the Gullah world

magically looms, under my lids,
as a bustling magazine:

not earnest *Ebony*, gossipy *Jet*,
or *Ladies' Home Journal*,

but like the lavish, brimming *Bon Marché*—
the French meaning of the word:

on the first floor,
a swift-as-a-robin runagate

trailing a fugitive-guiding star;
a stirring spectacle

of unfailing harvest women
fanning rice in round

winnowing baskets;
a coffle of chanting men

active in the sweat
of malarial Junes and Julys,

as summering rice kings
time and again consign them

to bullheaded sun,
unceasing swamp-labor

and unremitting malady—
On the second floor, a steely,

gray-eyed Gullah slave who endured
Job-and-Jonah-harsh snares

to savor a life, scot-free
of ironhearted masters,

blessing her uphill descendants,
still hardy, long-despised, still

winsome as luxuriant willows,
still abraded and believing in

the unkillable dream
of color-blind justice and respect—

On the last vaulted floor,
the ease and freedom

of nowadays, spread
like a vast fisherman's net

full of lost things and surprises,
like the reed-shifting ivory

of lithe herons lifting
from the marshland's darkening hem . . .

VII. Communion

A revering pitcher of milk
poured on a slave's

cool resting place
(even a ghost

needs sustenance, Augustus),
an artful Sea Island slave

christened Jupiter
who festooned his banjo

with crude, blue,
cantering horses,

a blinded slave who lived to savor
unbossed days.

My chains fell away:
that *dream.*

My chains fell away
with a Juneteenth glory.

*

In the midst of bondage,
ingenuity,

a deepdown plenty;
in the midst of plenty,

a glorious, saving
self-forgetfulness:

time spent with the bold-horsed,
at-the-ready banjo

roomed heaven time—
replenishing, redeeming,

warming him
as thoroughly as hoecakes

and the homeplace blue
of supper fires.

Likewise, in Carolina, a whole
dog day morning could be occupied

with the brusque wedding
of a disheveled wheelbarrow

and the windblown apples
from my grandfather's hardy trees.

*

Ghostyhead,
move-along man,

what is this night cousin to,
this Low Country night?

The onerous passage:
the well-deep dark of the hold,

the not-gutted baritone
crying and singing—

eoho, eoho—
of the man chained next to you—

as if God's Eden-intact fruit
were eternally out of reach,

as if solace and *dayclean*,
have mercy, were impossible:

dark of the hold
thick as blackstrap syrup.

*

Nevertheless, *dayclean* comes,
enlivening, bold as a posse,

with its buffer
of buttered cornbread,

of bracing coffee cooled
just so in a china saucer,

and hurried back to the cup
(my grandfather Frank's habit)—

Sustenance:
a shrimp-and-grits pipe dream,

then the real plate, oh my,
the real communion.

As if we could be fed,
washed clean, and crowned

with bride-gift shorebirds
(*that* dream),

all of our deeply stored wishes
waterborne, Augustus,

all of our derided people's
countless night terrors

hushed at last—whip-scars,
tears, and chimeras

of the slaveholding past
dissolved in *dayclean*'s

cleansing power, its pennant-clear
promise of resurrection.

*

On days of upending hunger,
breakspirit days,

able wrought-iron makers, able watermen
defer their dreams—

Heart, make room
for the blinded Gullah ghosts,

for the breadline men, make room
for the windfall apples.

19

VIII. *Caesars and Dreamers*

The pharaohs of rice and indigo, the conniving
Caesars of cotton,

what were we to them?
Profitable: able

bodies from Barbados
and the Windward Coast,

the Rice Coast,
our souls ramshackle,

less than a rooster's
or a rock's.

And yet, in painstaking fields,
in joyous praise houses,

our tenacious "Go Down, Moses,"
our stirring, rallying

"In the beauty of the lilies
Christ was born across the sea . . ."

might have served as proof
to those zealous Southern despots

that we possessed
some quilt scrap of God.

Go tell those greed-swayed
kings of sugar, those implacable

princes of tobacco,
how we garnered freedom

in our hardscrabble dreams,
sang it as sweat-drenched,

unshakable hallelujah,
whispered it as healing salve

to allay the defiling
stripes on our backs.

Unstinting overseer,
iron-eyed Caesar,

who better to define freedom
than a slave?

IX. Wild Indigo, Because

When rice was our nemesis
and callous-making cotton,

and the onus
of a Satan-hot tobacco

seemed to stain
our very souls,

beyond the spirit-choking
pesthouses of Sullivan's Island

(our Ellis Island),
beyond the dust and ragtag

squalor of slave row,
we found a dew-soaked,

purplish blue
in the needed time—

imagine,
in a siren patch

behind the blacksmith's—
a God-sent and doe-wild blue.

X. The White Iris Beautifies Me

Not the white of hard-won cotton,
or of pitiless snow—

I've found a whiteness
that gives me its glory;

it blooms
in Master Bellemare's garden,

and though it is, by all accounts,
untouchable,

quiet as it's kept, I've carried it
into the shabbiest of cabins,

worn it as I witnessed
the slave-breaker,

the hanging tree;
in dream-snatches

it blesses me, and I become
more than a brand,

a pretty chess piece:
at the mistress's bell,

always prudent and afraid,
wily and afraid—

And when the day comes,
my rescuing flower's name

will become my daughter's;
a freeborn woman,

I swear,
she will never be shoeless

in January snow.
Bold Iris,

she will never fear sale
or the bottom of the sea.

XI. Moon-Huggers

Amid cabin whispers of breakneck
runagates, invisible maroons,

wind-ferried Africans—
cornered, enchained, we let

magic become our ammunition:
from witnessing Carolina pines,

abetting bobwhites
reminded us, in forest code,

of the incantation tucked,
fail-safe behind our misery:

that at some unmanning moment,
we might rally and soar

from the tethering plantation
in one moon-hugging, star-scouting,

soul-of-a-nighthawk leap—
past sundering marketplaces,

bought & sold & bought & sold—
gliding east,

moon, moon, moon,
with an unpredicted glee . . .

XII. *The Abandoned Name*

In my salad days, Augustus,
flattering and fussing Sea Island folks

dubbed me Sheik,
and yes, my sent-away son,

the strut of it in a gimcrack world
was utterly clean:

Sheik the showstopper,
the unhurried sun

to sashaying girls—
coiled, flagrant, fatally cool,

brilliantined
to a fare-thee-well.

Siditty in blue serge.
Sheik of the Talented Tenth,

not one of those
feet-don't-fail-me-now men, surely,

not one of the sullied,
the unclaimed dead—

Nothing readied me
for Dachau—

not even a harassed boyhood
vexed by night riders,

redneck Furies,
crosses going up in flames.

Mass death made me
a neophyte again,

upbraided, throttled,
and dethroned me:

after the soul-cages of race,
the skin-and-bone men

behind barbed wire,
after Dachau, sheik of what?

XIII. Deacon Costen's Handclap Joy

Dozing near a welcoming blaze
of wild indigo,

I found little A.
in the woods out back,

and whipped him for the sissy-sweet
place he'd hidden . . .

But I was a wily truant,
full of escapades,

an under-the-Dipper dreamer
myself,

till, at fifteen, I felt
my pedestal-propped hero's lips

brush mine:
for a long time I believed

WWII made me into
a "lubricated" Low Country man,

but now I see:
the kiss was the screw-turn,

the kiss and the deepdown fear
ever after.

What else could have caused
my banishing of the boy

who spurred my hope of becoming
a soaring ace,

the boy so aptly named
Titus Sparrow—

who taught me to revere
the spirits of winged slaves.

But I declined his unbidden lips,
his beaming goodwill

and tales of thrilling magic.
He said he hadn't meant it

as a perverted thing,
scout's honor,

that I resembled a "red-boned"
angel in the hammock.

Time and again, time and again,
he begged to see me,

but I refused, till,
under some riverbank trees,

two startled anglers found
T.'s bloated body—

Lord, dear Lord, if I let
Augustus float away from me,

like Titus—if I called it sin
that separated us,

then I've lived to see my own sin
come to knock

at my upstanding door:
tight-lipped veteran,

deacon of the church,
on-the-sly drinker—

The old paint-by-numbers faith
seems puny now

beside the durable fire
of a thrown-away friend,

or a child's daydreamy pleasure
in a live-a-little bloom of indigo.

And the pay dirt
after decades of pain

is a handclap joy
like furious gospel,

as one man builds
the sturdy bridge back to his son,

one man soars away from
the secret glass at last.

XIV. I'll Take You to Africa

Daylean:
the telltale marshes

take the last gallivanting gold
and giveaway crimson,

and for a brief while,
quiet as it's kept,

even the sternest trees
seem to curtsy

and be set ablaze
by the razzle-dazzle sun's

adieu. After love's
bodacious vowels

and the agile sorcery
of dusk-sharing blackbirds,

it's this marriage of sundown hues
and marshland shadows

that moves us to speak.
High in a lark-haunted,

boy-loved oak,
one humming lover

soothes the other's
glistening nape

with a ham-shaped fan,
then whispers:

If you wear this ring,
I'll take you to Africa.

Two black men together make
a dipper-sweet singing,

a jump-the-broom bounty.
Daylean, daylean:

sun like a wedding cake
tucked beneath a pillow.

XV. *The Hurricane*

All the windows are open to the sea,
the murmur of Atlantic coral:

smash them,
smash them with your song,

wild to the Western ear—
And who are you,

with your stripping punches—
you're uprooting the palms,

you're tearing the leaves—
oh what you love is the skeletal—

and who am I,
that you would take my verdant snake,

my blessed island,
and dash it to pieces?

If this day, this aftermath,
is a thorny school,

the sere light and the day,
then what is the lesson in it?

That the gift is always imperiled?
That the swart, surviving horses,

the veteran palms seem
more alive now, more alive?

In the iron, gargantuan hush:
medicine and smithereens,

a fierce concentration
on cherishing the living.

From spirit back to spirit again;
dash it to pieces, Creator, Destroyer,

you pirate god, Huracán,
with your ferocious gangplank,

your pitiless and raucous
wind-that-will-ensure-grief—

And yet it dares to be born,
mud-fresh, mud-fresh,

like a foal,
amid the wreckage, the bankruptcy:

from spirit into flesh again:
resilience.

XVI. A Siren Patch of Indigo

Listen: though we swell as rampant
woodland or riverbank blossoms

(*Baptisia australis*)
in your tensile world,

as commonplace beauty
and reachable remedy,

as soothing eyewash for the Osage,
hardy dye for the Cherokee,

quiet as it's kept,
we're more akin to

clearing and hillside way-showers,
offhand griots quietly reminding you

the punishing rows, the grim
nightworld of the Middle Passage

was never your true province;
even in appalling chains,

the light of your integrity,
your inmost wonder

still encircled you,
resolute, inviolate.

Always recall, dear
progeny of Sea Island slaves,

in galling dearth
or in Juneteenth glory,

our deep, annealing, sacramental blue
belongs to you.

XVII. Itzak's Mighty Oak

As I was leaving Dachau,
that wild, raw negative of Eden,

a boy, thin as a wishbone,
scurried into my tank's path.

I halted, opened the hatch, and climbed out.
Clasping ragamuffin arms

around my regulation trousers, he raised
a tattered banner of English:

America!
Mickey Mouse! Mickey Mouse!

Augustus, I picked him up:
unmoored,

he might have been mine or even your
endangered son.

He marveled at my generous lips,
my nappy hair,

and Itzak made it bell-clear,
through his setter-eyed looks,

he'd never seen a Negro.
And in the proudest

moment of my life, I laughed and whistled,
content to be Itzak's mighty oak,

his at-the-ready knight
and his deliverance.

XVIII. The Gospel according to Wild Indigo

In time, the sea-loved Carolinas,
the spade-and-hoe land

which was our break-soul
yoke and lament,

became, so help us, our land.
On Lady's Island, Cat Island,

Daufuskie, St. Helena,
Ham's unlauded children,

broken and unbroken, we waded
in the mothering water,

garnering the Moses-wise
marshes' secrets,

the irrepressible crabs' broadcasts.
Under-the-Dipper dreamers, singers,

we let ancient oaks counsel us,
mossy Abrahams and Isaacs.

From pliant sweetgrass we coaxed
mint-new forms

of utility and beauty.
We learned resilience—

who better to define freedom
than a slave?—

a taproot waiting,
from the gospel according to wild indigo,

in which death and defiling
bondage are transformed

into foam and fish-scale blue,
a heron's swoop,

and bold-fisted hurricanes dismantle
the masters' belligerence—

Our prophet-smashing owners,
our slyly disowning fathers,

they told us we had no rights
to the dawn,

and gave us first instead
the gorgon's heart of the hold,

thick as blackstrap syrup.
But here it comes—

can we get a witness?
Here it comes,

with a runagate's swiftness—
eoho, eoho!—

night-yoked mother,
never-defeated brother, sister:

inspiriting,
down-to-the-wire,

immaculate
as a deacon's gloves·

dayclean.

II.
LOVERS BORROWING
THE LANGUAGE
OF CICADAS

Endless wealth,
    I thought,
        held out its arms to me.
A thousand tropics
    in an apple blossom.
        The generous earth itself
gave us lief.
    The whole world
        became my garden!
But the sea
    which no one tends
        is also a garden
when the sun strikes it
    and the waves
        are wakened.

—William Carlos Williams,
"Asphodel, That Greeny Flower"

RETURN TO FLORENCE

How do I convey the shoring gold
at the core of the Florentine bells'

commingled chimes?
Vast as a suddenly revealed

sea of wheat,
that up-and-away gold

is equivalent to the match-burst
morning I returned,

intent as doubting Thomas,
to my old classroom terrace,

open to the showy, blue *yes*
of the bustling Arno,

to my timeless, sun-laved
Basilica di Santo Spirito,

and discovered
ebullient citizens reciting,

at a hundred different posts,
the same unbetraying passage

of Dante's *Paradise.*

THE PINES OF THE VILLA PAMPHILI

Let me take you to my bodacious
roll call of pines,

a whole green legion of them;
colossal parasols, quelling sentinels;

they loom above the villa's
July paragraphs of purple blooms,

these salient but patient
titans of probity,

couriers that seem capable of revealing
time-out-of-mind keys;

listen, when the wind balks,
their keen caesura is the cool

hiatus, the hush of a Roman well's
rain-softened stone—

And when the breeze gusts
once more through this sublime,

Gulliver-sized army,
it's a mordant one, insinuating

even Odysseus had to forsake
his vintage sea and glistening Ithaca;

like tallow-pale Eurydice,
betrayed by a glance, he became

one of Death's possessions—
Yes, wind-voice in the villa grove,

brisk, telltale wind,
to be brutally honest, our love

for the bracing earth's
hard-to-pass-up pines,

consoling blossoms, and conveying seas
will never save us

from exodus,
transport from this world—

though all the while, the locomotive,
gloom-banishing blackbirds,

ensconced in the brilliant
choir stalls of cosmos,

keep insisting:
here, here—

ETHOS

Burly, storm-haired, semi-
miraculous, here's a seeker

in much-mended sackcloth,
rising from his discomfiting,

make-do bed, his marble bench
in the dove-white basilica's

galleon shadow—
There's an atavistic blaze,

an unbarricaded beauty
to his broken-toothed "*buona sera*"

and, when I hail him back,
a tightrope empathy,

as integral as a meticulous
clockmaker's oils—

our twilight exchange as unfussy
as the ethos of tonsured,

wolf-subduing Francis,
with his soul of a lighthouse rook,

yet, as I pass the Poor Clares
closing a heavy convent door,

as I wander Assisi's sinuous
salmon-pink alleyways,

up to the hilltop majesty
of its long-standing fortress,

the many-headed field,
rife with clover flowers,

masterless daisies,
I can't shake

the clarifying force
of the disheveled pilgrim's

shoeless humility—
migratory presence who makes

meant-to-crush-us poverty
and dreamt of bounty seem—

with the first arriving stars'
subtle orchestra—

suddenly fraternal,
like twin pepper and salt shakers

placed on a trestle table,
where a rapturous,

a timeless and appeasing feast
is slated to begin . . .

FEDERICO'S QUERENCIA

Take this dream-blown word,
querencia,

resilient as a thumb-worn rosary
or a cloud-cloaked seabird,

this lush equivalent
for the unlatched treasure trove

of up-to-the-minute dahlias
tucked under your star-guarded ledge,

the hope-granting anchor
of your climbable tupelo's

deepest taproot and heartening dove;
the fluent whispers of its familiar,

dizzy-making branches—the antithesis
of night raids, fusillades.

But *querencia*—transporting
as a loyal estuary,

luminous as the bones of saints,
also conveys the soul-steadying place

the beleaguered bull reveres,
seeks and reconnoiters

in the dead-sure arena
as sun-blanched, gritty Ithaca—

And like the animal,
hectored, yet emanating power,

claret-dark in the deterring ring—
Federico García Lorca,

the Andalusian sorcerer
of be-sure-to-use-your-eyes beauty

was brought to a dismaying end
by dawn marksmen as unerring

as any fabled picador
or applauded torero—

*

To embrace the word *querencia*
(like a coursing, fortifying

hearth-fire in my veins), I go
looking for sibylline Lorca's

long-fingered source, and find
his cradle in Fuente Vaqueros,

tobacco groves, curing houses,
sun-laved rows of artichokes, and still

quick-as-a-kestrel gypsies; I go
seeking his prized summer home's

deacon-straight palm,
and slipcovered piano;

when I touch the cover's
rose-and-beige paisley,

like a sly but fletcher-sure child,
I can't stop myself from envisioning

a mass grave blossoming
with impossible sharps and flats—

*

Through a little hullabaloo
of belled and bleating goats, I climb

from the bread-baking village
of demure Alfacar,

past robust pomegranates
and ripening figs,

past the wayfaring cobalt
of a thousand-year-old watercourse,

to the sobering barranca,
the wooded gully of Víznar,

where charismatic Federico
was emptied at sunup—

*

I know this: Federico's first paradise
was his sprawling *vega*,

the rustling, Zeus-high poplars
he addressed as a child,

imperial but giving poplars—
his gung-ho bastion

of glimmering autumn fields,
a boyhood stronghold

as pale yellow gold as *Idiazabal*,
a little block of Basque country cheese,

brought to my breakfast table—
I know this: it's piercing

to ford uphill to Víznar,
beneath the eremitic splendor

of the rocky outcrop,
to commit to full memory

lookout-vigilant pines
and immense hillside vistas;

piercing to imagine
the poet's Eden diminished

to a tumult of gunshots—

*

Under an end-of-summer sky, grown
pewter with the prospect of rain,

alert to the doleful pines'
Esperanto of soft keening,

in the grim-minded gully,
I become almost indivisible

from a dauntless song
that surpasses carnage,

a pressing wind
more ancient than David's harp—

*

Like a cogent guitar always opening
countless doorways:

Federico's *querencia*.

IN ROBERT GRAVES'S MALLORCAN GARDEN

Here the guileless breeze
in the placid orange boughs is buoyant

as a subway bootblack's whistle,
and I suddenly recall: floral scents

became unbearable aromas to Graves
in the first years following

the November armistice:
After breakspirit trenches,

red rows near the arbor
weren't allaying blooms at all

but foul mustard gas and morass . . .
And the lavish miracle

is how the upwelling seasons
ushered the distressed poet and fusilier

from the Great War's maiming
to the Valhalla of this island garden's

deep green parliament
of delectable branches—

Yes, far from aim and shell shock,
dear Robert,

deep in the safe-house beauty
of mist-shawled Deya,

there is no no-man's-land
under the orange leaves.

THE RED-HAIRED PUPPET

Say I sloughed off tenderness, playfulness
as a pipe-dreaming boy,

so my matchless odyssey
with the red-haired puppet, purchased

one rain-slick Parma morning,
took me by surprise.

On headlong trains, for weeks
I was an ally of the adept sun

and tallying wind,
the framed, wavering havens

of fast-glimpsed, exhilarating fields—
an unabashed witness

to an ever-shifting tableau,
an audience to the fullest diameter

of everyday eagerness,
shy blundering or brash posturing,

that displayed little difference between
motives and marionette strings—

In those mercurial spring weeks, I confess
my true companion

was of insouciant yarn
and artful papier-mâché,

little upbeat clown
with crescent-thin, caring eyes,

and I christened her in a daydream:
Antonella La Rossa—

Immodest Venice greeted us
with a double rainbow,

and the gingham-clad puppet,
all peach-colored, bruiseless hands,

seemed eager to applaud the city's
bonanza of showy beauty—

so like a sunburned Prospero,
a jubilant, just-washed-ashore magus,

with the supple, acceding wand
of welling hope,

I brought her to life.

THE SHADOW

after Hans Christian Andersen

Traveler, I came to a colossus
of clustered houses—a sultry kingdom,
replete with breeze-swept balconies,
belled donkeys, and vying boys
slyly triggering Roman candles—
all of it beneath a glittering
caravansary of detectable stars—

In the bullying heat
of that equatorial city,
my rambunctious shadow grew
thinner, desiccated, restless,
and leaped, abracadabra
(more jack-in-the-box
than agile gazelle!),
onto my mysterious neighbor's
intricate balcony.
When my rogue-swift, dark counterpart
returned, I asked:
What did you see? Who lives there?
Poetry, he revealed.
Yes, Poetry, as numinous and longed-for
as the northern lights,
often lives in palm-guarded places,
as a shuttered Garbo, an elusive
recluse cloistered among us—

Imagine: I was a seeker tantalized
by light and shadow
that I faithfully mimicked
in expressive oils and aquarelles,
an ardent, itinerant painter, attuned

to the way garden shadows
become diligent brushstrokes
or late afternoon lace.
So why should I be surprised
at my headstrong shadow?

After his first enlightening escapades
in Poetry's captivating rooms,
in one magnanimous gesture,
I set free my shadow to emerge
as his own up-and-coming man,
to acquire blue serge, a boutonniere,
a dapper bowler—
But he employed his newfound humanity,
his effusive charm and flair
to persuade the winsome princess,
my beloved fiancée,
that *I* was the unruly imposter, the mad
shadow who deserved oblivion:
first bedlam, then the chilly
volley of a firing squad—

And in the flash point I was manacled, I saw
our fierce mirroring was never
friendship, twinship,
but a crafty fisherman's net,
a supplanting spider's stratagem—I saw
how slowly and inexorably I became
a Christ in distress,
and my rebellious shadow
a charioteer, a ruffian god,
a key-cold executioner.

IF VAN GOGH DIDN'T SHOOT HIMSELF, WHO DID SHOOT HIM?

This isn't the castaway's story
that founders in a sea
of inglorious wheat, with a tempest
of tatterdemalion crows, the artful
passion that ends in self-injury:

In this reconstellated version
of Van Gogh's Calvary (the forensics,
two rebelling biographers claim,
aren't in sync with self-harm,
a secret long banished
by Auvers' abetting villagers),
maimed Vincent is nowhere near
the blistering wheat field
but on his way to abjure
the prince of a puffed-up band
of blithe pranksters, scheming,
blundering boys, all too happy
to deposit bedeviling pepper
on the Dutchman's brushes,
a jack-in-the-box snake
in his sibylline box of paints—

So hectored Vincent is set
on seeing the boys' ringleader, a wily,
be-my-guest sneak,
smug as a pickpocket, who dangles
his art-loving brother as bait
to torment the peculiar painter
the town delinquents nickname "Toto"—
Monsieur Rene Secretan, ready-set-go
in his outlandish costume
of fringed buckskin and chaps,

galling bully boy who models himself
a newfangled cowboy, a mock
Wild Bill Cody brandishing
a low-grade caliber pistol—

At the instant the feckless bullet,
intentional bull's-eye or misfired report,
finds beleaguered Vincent,
human scarecrow in harm's way
(far from a sureshot,
the green gunslinger dismantles
the oddball's summer day)—
oh he lets go, all at once,
a low-down, disgruntled vowel,
like the gasp of a herring-gull
grappling with the wind's gusto—

And vision's emissaries, transiting
cousins to the carrot-haired martyr's
once-requisite crows,
veer with the throttled black

of a hundred shuddering ministers—

TWO POETS QUARRELING UNDER THE JACARANDAS

I. The Quarrel

The Big Dipper spilling into a grammar
of almonds and valley wind,
muscatel and bougainvillea—
Near the lordly bell tower,
under the polestar rovers,
we were quarreling in the path
of billowing jacarandas—blue-violet shreds
italicizing the town walkways
under our moonlit sandals.
Half-drunk, en route to the hill
of the hard-at-work windmill,
dear ghost, tell me, what were we
at loggerheads about?
So help me, I can't recall—

Out of love, I'd come
to marvel at a Mediterranean Oz
of innumerable lemon rows,
to reach your family's finca
at the *tramuntana*'s hem,
where Flor, your mother, revealed
an infallible, carved eagle,
forever guarding your filigreed cradle—

That clashing moment
under the giveaway branches,
when your mutinous bangs erupted
over your brows,
your expressive mind racing past
your prepossessing body—
your suddenly unruly hair,
turned almost caution yellow

in moonlight and lamplight,
why is that the singular moment
I can't relinquish?
That's as real and vital to me now
as my gnarled hand
holding up a morning glory
in your boyhood garden,
fifty years after the revolution and civil war—

II. Carnival of Fire

Hard to believe, after half a century,
I'm here, relishing your Mallorcan home,
ensconced under another unbridled,
shedding, May-time jacaranda—
My able doctors insist I'm dying,
but what's death
after the doleful exodus of so many souls
during and following the civil war?
Your last surviving sister, Maria del Sol,
still witty and perceptive,
still unfettered in her approach
to Catalan life and politics,
not in the least provincial,
embraced me at the wrought-iron gate
but at supper, she whispered, slyly:

Batman and Robin,
Estragon and Vladimir,
Sancho and Quixote:
Half the island debated
if it was love, the pants-off kind!,
she laughed, *or merely friendship—*

So I ping-ponged back:
Mari, what do you believe?

I have my theories.
Wasn't it passion that turned you
into a poet?
An even greater one than him.
That had to be my brother's doing.
Possession almost!

I didn't answer your testing,
never-taciturn sister;
in mischief's name, she didn't expect,
much less require an answer;
I know, beneath it all, Maria was itching to ask:
Why did you lie and pretend
you visited him in the sanitorium,
when I know otherwise?
But even for her, there are limits
to her X-ray frankness—

So, as ever, I carried on, safeguarding
our youthful link, our secrets,
then segued into the lissome garden,
where, in lieu of your impassioned voice,
proclaiming, at the war's outset,
rage and bigotry
brought us to this bloodshed,
I heard heartening bells emit
from the mountain monastery,
the sound of cormorants' cries,
while the valedictory sun and headland sky
became an ecstatic carnival of fire.

III. Torch-Pass

Did your death stop my singing?
It did. For a dozen years, it's true,
no public performances
(underworld, chrysalis, total eclipse),
then I had Francesc and Lluc Maria fashion
fitting music for your poems—
the earliest ones evoking
port-of-call nets, pine-laden summits,
fields of shimmering olive and citrus,
and Lord, I was impelled, all systems go,
to sing again.
The infernal vortex, the battle between brothers
was a memory,
and marauding Franco's irascible ban
against our sacramental language
(Don't bark! Speak the language of the empire!)
began to loosen a little.
No, it wasn't adequate
to broadcast your captivating words
before a reverent crowd,
to eulogize your genius
in a candlelit island chapel
or a Valencia concert hall;
I was gripped by a galvanizing desire
to compose poetry as well.
A tenor and storytelling prodigy,
yet I'd never fashioned a single stanza
in the time preceding the war,
but after your upending death,
every word of our denigrated language
became precious ore;

in this torch-pass, I let go
interpreting bel canto and perfecting stories:

I became all poetry,
all silence and verse—

IV. The Keats Mirror

What god would make a Keats
and subtract his breath?
That's what you lamented
when we made our avid pilgrimage
to the "live-in-the-eye" poet's
narrow room, overlooking
the folderol of the Spanish Steps,
and when we gazed on the pauper's bed
where lamp-like John died
(at the very last, the prodigy's lungs
"completely destroyed,"
the whole flummoxed chamber
of his exhausted thorax
utterly blackened)—
we were mercifully undone and lucky
to mourn in peace for a while—

Then, worshipful students,
unflagging fans, we bought Parma violets
for the gone-too-soon poet's
innately humble grave,
beside the stone of his loyal helpmate,
Joseph Severn.
There in the lulling corner
near the cat-loved pyramid of Caius Cestius,
in the Protestant cemetery, we overheard
a little towheaded schoolboy ask,
And where is Mr. Keats?
In heaven?
And his fanciful mother answered:
I imagine he's on Hampstead Heath, son;
I imagine he's busy being a bee
or a nightingale—

In that Roman place of tranquil,
sun-reaching cypresses,
you shared the endearing tale
of a blissfully truant shepherd
that stalwart Severn once spied
dozing against the poet's grave—

And from the lofty but regretful
crow's nest of old age
and impending death
(Why do we love and fail?
Why are we meant to live and feel
the myriad ways we die?)
now I realize: you were my own
confounding Keats, my heart's crash
(who could have forecast
you'd suffer the nightingale poet's fate?),
but I was no wartime Severn
by your bedside—

V. The Hill of Muses

With our small coterie of dreaming-out-loud
scholars and writers,
we quit prodigal Rome and blatant Naples
for fabled Greece.
Though web-spinning Hitler, that master builder,
had wheedled his way to power
the previous winter,
on that intoxicating summer jaunt,
our own portable student world seemed
beautiful, impregnable—

In a downpour, we realized,
on the final dusk of our Aegean tour,
we were adjacent to Socrates's jail
and the panoramic Hill of Muses,
with its vista-facing tomb
of the great Roman consul Philopappos,
and in your weather-marred hat
and soggy, cream-yellow linen,
amid the stern pines, the soft bodies
of short-lived cicadas, you laughed
at the coincidence, insisting:
tempests, Mussolini—it's a messy world,
but wherever there's laughter, Salvador,
there's freedom—

Word-sorcerer, the way you saw it,
as tenacious Greek and Latin pupils
(all of twenty, tanned and resourceful
as stranded Crusoe and Friday,
those foraging castaways),
we reached back to the pagan
to find a puissant syntax to describe
all we meant to each other:

jejune seekers, atavists, strays
from the classical world;
in timeless Greece, we didn't need to label
our clandestine touching
as trespass, apostasy, or a Judas goat,
only tradition—

VI. Ashes and Jacarandas

In the dire war aria that begins
the terrible news continues,
the doctors detected TB,
and, with greyhound alacrity, at Three Kings,
you were gone: even younger
than your cherished Keats—

Forgive me, in that downfall winter
of meager rations, reliable bombings,
midway through the impinging war,
I couldn't reach the sanitorium in time,
so I had to envision (till I believed
wholeheartedly in the fantasy)
the hovering nurses, the frowning doctor
with his chilly stethoscope,
the final, apocryphal embrace—
elegizing your unbearable passing
in midlife verse, as if I had been there:
Lord help me, I wanted to be there,
to embrace you, yes—to hold even your urn
at the ash-gray end—

I lied, my poet, when I claimed
I couldn't pinpoint
the wellspring of our long-ago quarrel:
it was politics, of course, and more:
in the eleventh hour of the Republic,
in that engrossing chaos, that free-for-all
in which a man might be murdered
just for wearing a tie,
you'd urged us to flee the country,
and I had confessed, foolishly:
I couldn't imagine giving up Barcelona,
even for you . . .

In the island moonlight, you halted,
to emphasize your point;
your insurgent bangs cascaded
over your impressive forehead
and penetrating eyes,
then, all at once, you jettisoned
your fail-safe, wire-rimmed glasses,
and pulled my wary face to yours,
like a Roman or a Neapolitan!
Your near-kiss was the truce—
there, amid the frail firecracker shreds
of Mallorcan jacarandas,
where, in reverie or earnest prayer, I find,
as I move toward the dark frigate
of ever-demanding Death,
your point-blank beauty again . . .

PENTIMENTO

*Old paint on a canvas, as it ages, sometimes
becomes transparent. When that happens it
is possible, in some pictures, to see the original
lines: a tree will show through a woman's dress,
a child makes way for a dog, a large boat is no
longer on an open sea.*

—Lillian Hellman

Once upon a time, he was waiting,
his desire almost visible,
like a lovely spider's thread
undulating in the morning sunlight,
and the lag-time seemed
interminable, stifling
as a meddlesome chaperone
or a nosey, stiff-necked matron—
waiting, in fact, for his freckled,
no-longer-kite-flying soldier
to return on furlough—alert,
almost on tenterhooks
for his sly, trespasser's whistle,
so the two (unmonitored lovers)
could relish, all by themselves,
the whole, blissfully fragrant copse,
the sleepy-eyed, anonymous pond
they loved to splash and sputter in
as raffish boys,
where the accidental brush of their thighs,
at fourteen and fifteen,
became a match-flare—

Looking with intent, keen-eyed care,
at this aging canvas, it's clear
the fabled, pewter-eyed painter "repented":

Banished, the coal-black
of the far-off bell tower,
and the first, emboldening road;
vanished, the saffron yellow
of the breeze-swayed field,
ready to absorb the artist's
very first grief—first sobs
like broadcast vestiges of wind
on gilded blue pond water—

Once upon a time, he was waiting
and the doleful news of Alessandro's arrest
didn't reach him for days,
foolish Sandro, once a marvel
of high jinks and horseplay, who imagined
a ticktock life in the barracks
would make him more of a man,
instill in him
his captious father's ideals,
but that out of the blue yen
to master discipline backfired,
for his commanding sergeant
nudged him almost daily
for "a little sweet and spice,"
so that in the gruff, manly barracks,
Alessandro longed for the painter.
And when the cajoling sergeant dared
to caress his pale skin in secret,
as he dozed in his upper bunk,
hectored, startled-awake Sandro
struck him,
and the unchecked lecher died
headfirst in the fall.
Oh Alessandro—the hawkish police
had him in paining handcuffs,
before he could reach

the ardent blue and green music
of their agreed-on pond—

That's why the downcast colors
of the second palette
are almost caustic, miserly, immuring
the original lines that implied
hope braided with hard-to-hide
passion, never lurid crime
and dispiriting ambush;
why, in the altered painting,
renamed *The Capture*,
the unmarred red of poppies
in the mummified layer, makes way
for fugitive Sandro's outsized,
faintly crimsoned fingers,
and the guileless green
of their getaway copse,
the consecrated green, is still visible
under the brackish costumes of the stern,
apprehending police—

And true, viewer, as you might guess
from this revelatory pentimento,
from the silver-haired painter's
prevailing choice:
because of the scandalous trial,
the gray, austere prison years
that came of it,
oh, he never saw Sandro again—

MASSIMO AND SILVER

I. Identical

When I came back for Massimo,
twenty years had passed:

the brash sea
was the selfsame turquoise,

the same brisk, unceasing spool
below the promontory;

the uncountable roof tiles
of the seafront city

(made tiny by the dizzying cliffs),
the identical terra-cotta—

II. Massimo and Silver

True: the lustrous hillsides,
the colossal bell tower

remained uniform, unchanged,
but Massimo himself was no longer

the unblinking, sun-marked Sicilian
who gladly escorted me

from a bygone hermitage
to Diana's broken temple—

I spotted poignant silver, spilling
from his blue and poppy tank top,

cheering threads of silver, scattered
pell-mell in his cascading hair—

III. Indelible

Tell me, Mr. Mystery, did we ever reach
Diana's temple?

Massi, I can't recall—
But what's indelible, of course,

is the long-ago 5 PM
when the college sophomore

offered me a peach
from his faded rucksack,

his ancient-as-Eve lure
to risk a man's whiskery kiss

for the first time, savoring,
with a cardsharp's or a mint-new

Casanova's aplomb,
bits of delectable pulp

from my juice-stained fingertips—

IV. The Core

He's vanished,
the impetuous Virgil I adored,

my unhindered pilgrim,
but on the promontory,

an up-to-the-minute Massimo
affords me a felicitous smile, pleased

with the lingering tern's cameo,
the playful gust's finesse:

proof of unremitting Time's
lust to alter form

but never the exhilarating core—

JASMINE

These are the days of jasmine in Rome—
when headlong, emboldened April has dissolved,

and the joyous braiding of sun and rain
brings this sweet, steady broadcast;

when I step from the suppertime train,
that's what greets me:

Roman hedges and walkways,
graffiti-laden precincts graced

with pallid fireworks, so even
the most tumbledown niches seem

breeze-swept,
festive now with fragrance—

Jasmine—the elating moment's shibboleth,
the cool, enrapturing night's cavalry—

Even crone-glorious Daria,
my terrace-loving neighbor, confides:

When Galliano came back from the front,
his right hand was bandaged,

but in his uninjured one,
ah, poet, he held

a fistful of jasmine he'd picked
along the path to my door.

How could I not become his wife?

LOVERS BORROWING THE LANGUAGE OF CICADAS

No one would suspect from the cicadas' cries
they're on the verge of dying.

—Bashō

That plate-smashing, ladder-to-the-moon
summer you first shadowed me

through my sea-lit hotel's
innocuous corridors,

down to the inlet, and I grasped
it was no mere coincidence

(well, I'd never have imagined you
a lover of men),

I told myself to memorize
all the deluxe lights

of the boisterous dance hall,
the canopy of attention-getting stars,

and even now, decades later,
I can summon them

nearly at will: balm
of the emboldening evening air,

glory-bound clouds,
blanched further by the immoderate moon—

No rhyme or galvanizing reason why
almost every afternoon

we beat an unfailing route,
past the frail but cordial puppet seller,

through the sun-bullied park,
through a barrage of voluble cicadas—

bristling and wild as mayhem
but truer than that—

as if their unbridled strains
were nimbly revealed,

sim sala bim,
as our own maverick vocabulary—

In Hersonissos, when we flourished,
minus any shared language,

no scaffold of expressive Greek
or all-conquering English,

only hasty drawings on a pad
and pressing gestures of desire—

I swear I didn't know
you had a kept-quiet wife,

a luckless child on the way
(a stillborn son),

so when I consider, inter alia,
your coppery beard,

your wine-soaked tongue
laving my young man's body,

lanky and elegant as a kouros,
in glimmering coves

and hideaway olive groves,
my body, once skittish and bronzed

by Crete's commanding sun,
I want to strike out

those Aladdin's carpet escapades
like glaring errors,

because a lie is a lie
in any language,

even the cicadas'—

THE SIBYL'S SONG

All sunny majesty, the sibyl's island
is far more than just

a sailor's braggadocio
or a reflexive dreamer's hyperbole:

four million almond trees in bloom
equal four million epiphanies—

When Mallorca's forever apt,
close-at-hand almonds

are a winter-buried fire,
at the altar of an outlying church,

a soprano with a consecrated sword,
intones an unsettling, long-sung page

of the apocalypse, to spellbound
magi of shimmering scales

and sun-dried nets,
who wouldn't exchange the sibyl's

Christmas Eve clarity
for all the sea's blue bullion—

The hallowing sibyl
is hope and altitude,

prayer-glow and holiday warning,
her transfixing voice, floating

above the timeworn pews,
the wood-carved, shining

newborn in the lowly manger,
as deep dark

as a shipwreck's blurred hull—
When the riling southern wind,

called *xaloc*, assails the Balearic coast,
leaving capsized boats and scurrying

battalions of fish,
the lure of the sibyl's

knife-clean December singing
leads the sanguine villagers,

the hectored fishermen to imagine
their souls might be enhanced

by even their storm-broken oars,
even the briefest beauty.

ANTINOÜS

at Hadrian's Villa

The siesta-hour beauty of his body:
even the villa olives are envious,

and the pensive sun, imagine,
and the vying poppies—

See how remarkably
his signature, tallied curls,

and sconce-intense eyes
have come down to us,

in expressive statuary and hardy coins—
We've been hearing lavish tales

of lithe Antinoüs's glory
(the lover made into an upraised star)

and the emperor's boundless loss
for some time now.

Have we learned a little
about toppling desire? Unchecked love

raised to the level of the gods?
Like chiding Clement of Alexandria,

feel free to ask the illustrious
but ensnared Hadrian's ghost:

Why magnify his beauty?
Why count among the deities

one prized merely
for his pleasure-giving nights and days?

Resplendent as a winning chariot
come to rest,

Antinoüs is not ambition, not decorum, not sanity:
trim Antinoüs's kingdom

is the alluring terra of a lover's
moonlit, ineluctable arms—

Does it matter if Hadrian's favorite
drowned by accident

or by his own hand?
The impinging sorrow's nearly the same:

wine-sweet Antinoüs means
the chilling assurance,

merciless as a corsair,
we will love and lose

as surely as effusive summer will segue
into inconsolable fall's

shower of sun-gold leaves . . .

NECROPOLIS

There's an immense veil of dust remaining
from a retinue of just-passed horses.
Near rain-sullied tombs,
brindled and voracious goats,
with their sly animus
of *I still, I still, I still,*
forage in the wayside grasses—
Amid a breeze-swayed mix
of Queen Anne's lace and fragrant fennel,
a pale, agile mongrel appears,
beneath the lowering sun,
and follows me
on the hoof-marked path, an affable
opposite of Cerberus,
lightening my impromptu odyssey
through the poppy-lit necropolis.

In this hour of seguing,
late spring light, at the Etruscan ruins
called Banditaccia—
mosaic, puzzle, juggernaut, queen—
having spied the official site's
locked, taciturn gate, I'm happy to find,
as I amble in Cerveteri's
cost-free, adjacent countryside,
tomb after empty tomb:
most coal-dark or genesis-dark,
some rank with bullying weeds
or brackish water—
Relentlessly, over centuries,
sagacious tomb raiders,
rogue-hearted plunderers have ransacked
the consecrated houses of the dead,
absconding with the earnest mourners'

devotional gold and bolstering trinkets,
little bronze ships of death
meant to ease the beloved's journey
from the wheat-bold kingdom of the *campagna*
to the underworld's
evening-cool, immutable ebony—

Know that we're eluding
the humdrum, the everyday,
my plucky anti-Cerberus and I.
Passing from womb
to rock-cut womb,
easy-footed yet intent, riveted—
in this subterranean silence,
I'm suddenly reminded
my mother succumbed to leukemia
during my last Italian sojourn
(there was, I swear, an imposing
volume and sweetness
to her scattered ash and bone
as I shared her with the living ocean's
teal artillery)
so truly now, I'm keener-eyed,
more acquainted
with elegy and chiaroscuro,
even able to surrender
something of her instilling light
and let it be subsumed,
at the sun's disappearance,
into Banditaccia's gargantuan stone
paean to the irreplaceable—

I admit: a venerating city of the dead,
designed for the living, seems
a massive courtesy, a loving-kindness,
and if, in this long-standing necropolis,

I brush against the limitless unknown
of my own mortality, my mother's
(one generation vanishing into another),
I'm also in sundown dialogue with you,
distant Etruscans—you who signal
to our deracinated age
in forlorn shards and intriguing frescoes,
you whose language is revoked, dismasted—
Were your lives like chalk equations
erased from a schoolroom blackboard?
Or do you truly dwell
in the jeweled realms of the perpetual?

Here, where the selvage-shorn day's
leave-taking light
feels like dying,
and night's voluminous toga arrives,
we remain, as in vanished Etruria,
brash and callow, ardent and in a hurry,
avid for heart-granting clarity and inheriting
mainly reticence and darkness,
though we have the sweeping beauty
of the coruscating here and now
for consolation, the heart-shoring
meshes of the migrant stars—

Here, where we're first mothered
and then unmothered,
monitoring spirits of the looted tombs,
here on indomitable earth,
with its safekeeping dogs
and timeless stone testaments,
we still seek news of you.

LAZARETTO

In Trieste one sultry July I stayed
on "Old Lazaretto,"

a long port street that the adroit poet
Umberto Saba revered.

Lazaretto, the locals informed me,
means the behemoth

of a brick hospital,
shipshape for the moribund

as well as a severe, quarantined boat,
a gray-souled station

for foundering seafarers—
Ambling the adjacent harbor, I faced

an open stretch of sea,
tranquil, stately beyond belief,

a blue, allaying mirror,
but I never encountered

a guide willing to impart
the origins of the old lazaretto,

a soul able to usher me
to the actual site, where Death prevailed,

tireless as a forest partisan—

*

At final count, eleven funeral parlors
refused his beloved's body,

so harried Raphael was charged
to hurry it into earth on his own;

granted, that was at the onset
of the winnowing AIDS years—

remember?—
when no physician could discern

the source of the ambushing disease.
It wasn't just disgust, all-out disavowal

that made the wary shunt
the stricken men with garish lesions:

fear is the quickest contagion—

*

*Lazar house, pesthouse,
and in its most musical form, lazaretto—*

Listen, in those lazaretto years
of fraught cell counts, mounting pills,

and spiraling hospices, rife
with featureless walls, I recall:

the tame and mannerly
failed us, yes, timidity and etiquette,

that Romulus and Remus,
were wholly decimated,

so that we were cast adrift, bereft
of any steadying map

or outright destination,
though, to be solicitous,

we were inclined to ask:
What are you feeling?

How are you today?
Then the answer might come

from a downcast "disco Apollo,"
or even your dearest friend,

a dancer/choreographer barely thirty,
reliant suddenly on an ominous cane

because his once expressive legs
were collapsing—

*

Hear me, when myriad, no longer hale
men left us,

and my bustling "City by the Bay,"
the city that thrilled us,

became a lazaretto,
I was a first-time lover,

a questing seeker
in the first months of outbreak,

of mystery and runaway mourning—
I speak for the shattered,

the aggrieved but still-alive,
the voluminous missing,

when I say once more:
Fear is the quickest contagion—

I can't believe I survived.

SPRING AND THE SPIRIT OF SAINT JOAN

In that rushing, animate place
where Saint Joan bent and slipped

from the bustling river,
illiterate but immense

peasant girl with her mystic banner,
I bent down, as if to grasp

the gadabout current's force, the dauntless
horses of her ambition—

An unnerving surfeit of storm-ridden,
harridan days in Burgundy

tested the shut-in villagers'
rough-hewn souls and stamina,

but winter's fierce marathon
was nothing compared to the grieving mind's

marksmanship, the flummoxed heart's
quest. In that Norse-cold,

unremitting kingdom, hungry for light,
avid for crocuses, I could have used

the girl-dressed-as-a-man's
clear-eyed faith and helmet—

Dear armored dreamer,
I thought I couldn't bear

another scourging rain,
another friend's death,

but here are the late-arriving leaves
emblazoning the prayer-path,

the enthralling blossoms
in the priest's vaunted orchard,

crowding my vision all at once—

A TALE OF TWO HIKERS

Often there were eye-catching poppies
along the train tracks—

Sky-opened and sea-opened,
in Manarola, I'd follow

the steep, rain-freshened way
of wild red valerian

and light-trapping lemons,
to the lofty, cached-away

village of Volastra,
then down to the scenic

cliffside paths:
Green-garbed May was the ideal time,

the ideal temperature for hailing
the sea's laudable glamour—

In tranquil Corniglia, I relished
the horizon's final, heart-quickening

portions of available light—sudden
pennants of sumptuous peach,

clerical red, and sublime purple—
sharing those precipitous colors

with a genial stranger, still elated
from his coastal trek.

Below our enlivening
cat's cradle of revealed connections,

the jutting rocks, the blue dories,
and the sea's austere jewelry

all began to glow and dull
in the swiftly amassing

day's end. When we both confessed
our irrecoverable parents

(both of us had lost,
first our industrious fathers

then our shrewd mothers) were still
fallible and potent, still crackling,

deepdown, under our lids,
we were rung like a dusk-lit

campanile's black bell.
And then our human joy,

laced with an ageless grieving,
our obvious fatigue

from the strenuous up-and-down
between villages,

our slowing, May-time voices
were hushed by the dark-at-last

tide's acrobatics,
by the rampant, inspiriting

prophet-sound of the sea . . .

ELEGY WITH A GOLD CRADLE

Now that you're forever
ministering wind and turquoise, ashes

eclipsed by the sea's thrust
and the farthest tor

(I know you were always
more than my mother)—

giveaway flecks tipped and scattered
from an island palisade—

Now that you're a restless synonym
for the whistling fisherman's

surfacing mesh,
the alluring moon's path and progress

through a vast chaos
of unrelenting waves,

let me reveal:
in the at-a-loss days

following your scattering,
in my panoramic hotel, I found

a sun-flooded cradle—
so pristine, so spotlit and sacramental

beside my harbor-facing bed,
I couldn't bear to rock

or even touch it, Mother:
I marveled at the gold-leafed bars

and contours—the indomitable,
antique wood beneath, an emblem

of unbeatable hope
and prevailing tenderness—

then, for a crest-like, hallowing hour,
listen, my mourning was suffused

with the specter of your lake-calm
cascade of hair, inkwell-dark

in the accruing shadows,
your rescuing, soothing contralto,

and oh yes, Isabel,
the longed-for fluttering

of my nap-time lids:
entrancing gold

of the first revealing dawns,
the first indispensable lullabies—

ACKNOWLEDGMENTS

My deep gratitude to my dynamic editor, Jon Tribble; to my spirited and shoring Cave Canem community of poets; to Ann Harper for making my visits to Charleston over the years so rich and interesting; to the Lannan Foundation for a resident fellowship; to the National Endowment for the Arts; and to Texas State University for providing me with an academic leave to finish this book.

My love and kudos to Veronica Golos, Ellen Hinsey, and Suzanne Gardinier, who taught me the word *querencia*.

My hearty thanks to the editors of the following journals and anthologies, in which these poems first appeared, some in earlier versions: *Academy of American Poets Poem-a-Day, African American Review, AGNI, AMP, Angles of Ascent: A Norton Anthology of Contemporary African American Poetry, Arts and Letters, Bearden's Odyssey: Poets Respond to the Art of Romare Bearden, Best American Poetry 2017, Callaloo, Cape Gazette, Cortland Review, Delaware Poetry Review, The Good Men Project, Gulf Coast, Icarus, Literati Quarterly, Nine Mile, Pluck!, The Ringing Ear: Black Poets Lean South, Salmagundi*, and the *Taos Journal of International Poetry and Art*.

"Federico's Querencia" is dedicated to Sarah Arvio.

The question "who better to define freedom / than a slave?" in "Caesars and Dreamers" is from an interview with novelist John Edgar Wideman in the PBS documentary series *Africans in America*.